Daumier and Music

Et. CARJAT.

H. DAUMIER

Daumier and Music

60 PRINT REPRODUCTIONS

COMPILED AND WITH AN INTRODUCTION BY

EGON GARTENBERG

DA CAPO PRESS • NEW YORK • 1992

Library of Congress Cataloging in Publication Data

Daumier, Honoré, 1808-1879.
  Daumier and music: 60 print reproductions / with an introduction by Egon
Gartenberg.
      p.   cm.
  ISBN 0-306-76054-1
  1. Music in art. 2. Music—France—Paris—19th century—Caricatures and
cartoons. 3. French wit and humor, Pictorial. I. Gartenberg, Egon. II. Title.
ML85.D34 1992   90-22964
741.5'944—dc20   CIP

The 58 lithographs and two woodcuts in this collection were originally
published between 1833 and 1871 in various Paris periodicals, notably
Le Charivari, La Caricature, Le Petit Journal pour rire and *Le Journal
amusant.* The captions have been translated into English for this volume.

Introduction © 1992 by Belle Gartenberg

Published by Da Capo Press, Inc.
A Subsidiary of Plenum Publishing Corporation
233 Spring Street, New York, N.Y. 10013

Publisher's Note

The original French captions and headings for the sixty plates that follow have been freely translated, to match Daumier's colloquial style. The editors are indebted to Jacques Barzun for his indispensable counsel in capturing the subtleties of Daumier's meaning and clarifying obscure contemporary references.

The plate numbers cited, as well as the date and place of initial publication, are from the ten-volume *catalogue raisonné* of Honoré Daumier's lithographs by Loys Delteil, published in Paris 1925-1930. Dimensions are in millimeters, the first figure representing height and the second width.

Preface

The art of Daumier has experienced a renaissance in recent times. Why does Daumier appeal so strongly to our generation as well as to his own? If we were to sum up his appeal in two words, they would be "timeliness" and "timelessness." The introduction to the illustrations in the present collection examines the human, social, and artistic factors in Daumier's achievement.

This volume deals with Daumier's graphic works on music and musicians. While certain of his plates, such as *The Lawyers,* have always been popular, the approximately seventy lithographs that deal with or allude to music and musicians are less known, never having been collected in volume form. Most of the lithographs presented here were reproduced directly from the original *Le Charivari* pages. In some instances newsprint from the obverse page has bled through, and the reader's indulgence is requested.

I wish to thank the following institutions and individuals for their valuable assistance and cooperation:

> The Print Collection of the New York Public Library
> The Baltimore Museum of Art
> The Boston Art Museum
> The Fogg Museum of Harvard University
> The Art Museum of Smith College
> The National Gallery, London
> M. LeComte, Paris

My personal thanks to Elizabeth Roth, Keeper of the Prints, New York Public Library, for her advice and guidance in my search for specific prints; to Dr. Francis Hyslop, Professor Emeritus of the Art History Department of the Pennsylvania State University, for his reading of the manuscript and his valuable suggestions and corrections; to Dr. Irma Smith of the Mont Alto Campus of the Pennsylvania State University, for help in translating the original French texts; to Marjorie Blubaugh, Assistant Librarian of the Mont Alto Campus of the Pennsylvania State University, for her aid in research; and to my wife Belle for profound moral support.

E.G.

Introduction

Honoré-Victorin Daumier was born in Marseilles 26 February 1808, but he was a product of Paris. Influenced by his dreamer-poet father and his practical mother, he was an outwardly conventional revolutionary who expressed his ideals in his art; a quiet, resourceful man amid revolution, war, and violence—the July upheaval of 1830, the 1848 revolution, Louis Napoleon's coup d'état of 1851, and the Franco-Prussian War of 1870.

Daumier's first teacher, the renowned painter and archaeologist Alexandre Lenoir, introduced him to the art of Michelangelo, Rembrandt, Rubens, Tintoretto, and other masters in the Louvre. From Charles Philipon, he soon learned the technique of lithography, which was quicker, more direct, and less expensive than painting. Invented in Germany in 1789 by Aloys Senefelder, lithography thrived in Paris from 1815. Delacroix, Ingres, and the exiled Goya were among the notables who studied the new art form.

Philipon became the journalistic inspiration behind Daumier. A master of political caricature, he foresaw the impact lithographic cartoons could have on the public's continuing hope for freedom from Louis Philippe's harsh rule. In 1830 he founded the journal *La Caricature* with his brother-in-law, the printer M. Aubert, and hired Daumier to draw the cartoons. Two years later he began a second journal, *Le Charivari*. Both were dedicated to "warfare every day upon the absurdities of every day." *La Caricature* withstood almost five years of fines, threats, and jail terms caused by its snarling wit and biting sarcasms. *Le Charivari,* on the other hand, survived for decades with its special brand of satire and caricature. Contributing a full-page cartoon to each issue, first of *La Caricature* and then of *Le Charivari,* Daumier became the master of the political cartoon.

La Caricature's influence increased as political conditions in France deteriorated. With each issue the text and the illustrations of Daumier and the other lithographers on the staff became bolder in their attacks against the king, the prime minister, the legislative body, and the police. The police began to seize entire issues, confiscate or destroy the stones, and threaten court action and jail. In retaliation, Philipon transformed the head of Louis Philippe step by step into the shape of a pear. The symbol represented Louis Philippe so successfully that Daumier hung the king in effigy by stringing up *La Poire* (D 47).[1] Other caricaturists on the staff took up the symbol, and the king saw La Poire everywhere. *He* was reported to have smiled, but not his entourage. In January 1832 Philipon was remanded to Sainte-Pélagie prison. *La Caricature* intensified its satire, causing the police to seize the stones and prints of Daumier's popular new image of Louis Philippe, *Gargantua,* which portrayed the king seated on a movable toilet. Court indictments followed swiftly, and Daumier, convicted of fomenting disrespect and hatred against the king and His Majesty's Government, was imprisoned at Sainte-Pélagie for six months.

During Daumier's prison term, Philipon founded *Le Charivari.* The title means "hubbub, clatter, noise, uproar" (Cassell); more specifically, "tumultuous noise of pots and pans accompanied by cries in whoops, made before the house of those who have incurred displeasure" (Larousse). The woodcut strip of the new journal showed Philipon beating a drum inscribed *Le Charivari.*

Upon his release, Daumier turned on the men who had persecuted him. *Masks of 1831* (D 42) and *The Legislative Belly* (D 131), two of his early masterpieces, are forceful and to the point. For *The Legislative Belly* Daumier had fashioned his famous "faces in clay"—small busts of unbaked clay, probably suggested by Philipon—before drawing them on stone. These busts, of which only thirty-seven were preserved by recasting into bronze, show him as a sculptor as well as a lithographer.

Philipon and Daumier had chosen their targets with ingenuity and force. Louis Philippe was no longer amused; the vicious cycle of print, publication, raid, seizure, and trial was proof of the two men's accurate aim. To raise badly needed capital, Philipon formed a print-of-the-month club. Some of Daumier's contributions were so masterful that the king's anger forced the club to shut down. One of these prints, *The Funeral of Lafayette* (D 134), exposed the king's hypocrisy with full satiric force, his face half smiling behind his folded hands as the cortege passes in the background. Another print was one of the triumphs of Daumier's life, *Rue Transnonain* (D 135). After a tenant had shot and wounded a gendarme, the police broke into the house at 12 Rue Transnonian and murdered its inhabitants. Only Goya's *Executions of 3 May* and Picasso's *Guernica* can compare in depicting cold-blooded slaughter. The print caused a sensation in Paris. The government retaliated swiftly by confiscating the stone and all remaining copies, and by holding a mass trial of all 121 men who had been involved in the 1834 riots. It was farce: The 121 prisoners were condemned by 164 judges. Daumier again protested eloquently, in the face of gag rules and death

---

[1]Lithographic references are to Loys Delteil's catalogue of Daumier's work (Paris, 1825-30).

threats, in his lithograph, *Go ahead and speak, you are free, you have the floor* (D 116).

An attempt on the life of Louis Philippe provided the excuse the king had been waiting for. He emerged unharmed, but fourteen Parisians died. The government forced the much-persecuted republican paper *La Tribune* to close. On 9 September 1835, the Assembly decreed that no sketch, lithograph, or other emblem could be published, shown, or sold. Philipon closed *La Caricature* with a reference to Lamartine's phrase, "the reign of terror of ideas." The issue contained Daumier's print, *They certainly had a lot of trouble killing us* (D 130)—a variant on the ancient gladiators' greeting to Caesar ("we who are about to die salute you"), as three men killed in the revolutionary struggle rise from their graves.

For the next thirteen years the satirists of *Le Charivari* were politically gagged. Since he could no longer caricature the king, Daumier used his crayon to lampoon Paris itself, a city which saw its commoner king, in top hat and umbrella, frequenting the streets that glittered with elegant restaurants and new theaters, yet which kept intact its caste system of nobility, literati, nouveau riche, and bourgeoisie. Daumier received most of his inspiration from the east side of Paris, the Faubourg Saint-Antoine. There he did not look for satire or polemic but for identification with the strata of artists and artisans, peddlers, street musicians, and barkers, those forgotten people who densely populated the narrow, reeking alleys and backwaters. Amid these extremes, the nobility and the nouveau riche on the one hand and the little people on the other, vegetated the bourgeoisie, which soon became the target of Daumier's social caricature. The bourgeoisie resisted all efforts to change it, caring nothing for the arts or the intellect, living its daily routine through cunning and scheming, bowing to those above it, kicking at those below it. Balzac all but championed these types in his *La Comédie humaine*. Daumier exposed them with a clear eye and inexhaustible curiosity, inspiring Baudelaire's comment, in *The Mirror of Art:*

> Look through Daumier's work and you will see parading before your eyes all that a great city contains of living monstrosities in all their fantastic and thrilling reality.

The change from political to social satire was at first difficult for Daumier, who contented himself in the beginning with directing a feeble wit at Parisian types (D 260-270). Philipon adjusted more quickly. As he had created La Poire to symbolize previous years, he now created Robert Macaire. The king was inviolate, but his regime, its wiles, greed, corruption, and incompetence, were not. Through this new symbol Philipon and Daumier could indirectly attack the king. Robert Macaire was not their creation. He had appeared on stage as early as

1823: a scoundrel, wise to the ways of the world, ready to exploit others and survive. By 1834 he had become a stage success. Daumier made Macaire the opportunistic symbol of his day. In one hundred prints between 1836 and 1838 he explored and exploded the France of Louis Philippe, the mores and manners of the bourgeoisie, in the figure of Robert Macaire the promoter and his unscrupulous schemes. If Macaire wore the same battered hat as Louis Philippe, the Parisians smirked and understood, and the censor was powerless. Daumier opened the historic series with *I Adore Industry* (D 354), one of the few examples where Philipon's text is as important as Daumier's drawing, as Robert addresses Bertrand:

> I adore industry. If you wish we will start a bank, a real bank. Capital: one hundred million dollars, and one hundred million billion shares. We will smash the Bank of France, we will sink the bankers, the charlatans, we will sink everybody.
> Yes, but what about the police?
> How stupid you are! Does one ever arrest a millionaire?

The artistic climate had begun to change from royally approved topics such as David's *Cupid and Psyche* to the romantic realism of Géricault's *The Raft of the Medusa* and Delacroix's flamboyant drama *The Massacre of Scio*. However, amidst hundreds of mediocre Salon entries the young malcontents, Daumier among them, were not yet accepted, and their work was called "frightful," "absurd," and "barbarous." At the same time, Victor Hugo's romanticism was emerging in literature and Hector Berlioz's in music. The word "romantic" in nineteenth-century music, though not explicitly political, stood for rebellion against many aspects of the classical style—formalism and lack of passion among them. Beethoven, the rebel of the *Eroica,* had been the idol of the young romantics; Berlioz took up the cause of romanticism in music after Beethoven.

The theater was also embroiled in the battle of new versus old. Auber, Bellini, Donizetti, Meyerbeer, and Rossini were the rage in opera, while Racine, Corneille, and Molière dominated the theater together with Dumas père, Scribe, and Victor Hugo. Daumier enthusiastically depicted the theater from both sides of the footlights. But the bourgeoisie viewed all attempts at renewing France's artistic spirit as vulgar, eccentric, or capricious. It was mainly France's young republican wing who championed Delacroix and consigned Ingres to the past.

If only a small minority dared to appreciate Delacroix's rebelliously flamboyant art, fewer still approved of caricature. While they laughed at Daumier's cartoons, the thought that they were also viewing art never occurred to them. His time had not yet arrived. Depressed although not discouraged, Daumier turned to oil painting as a relief from the drudgery of weekly cartoons, with Delacroix's *Liberty Leading the People* his inspiration. Delacroix, in turn, pinned his young admirer's lithographs to his studio walls. Daumier also did wood engraving, his work in this genre evoking comparisons to the master productions of Dürer and Holbein. But lithography gave the most successful expression to his satire.

In 1840 Philipon sold *Le Charivari,* but Daumier continued his social satire for the journal with a series of lithographs, *Histoire ancienne* (D 925-974), attacking the fad of neoclassicism in furnishings and on the stage. Baudelaire was one of the few who understood, as expressed in *The Mirror of Art:*

> The *Histoire ancienne* . . . seems the best paraphrase of the famous line "Who will deliver us from the Greeks and the Romans?" Daumier came down brutally on . . . false antiquity . . . He snapped his finger at it . . . a farcical ugliness which is reminiscent of those decrepit old tragic actors.

Histoire ancienne had to wait until eighteen years after Daumier's death before it received an honorable mention in the Goncourts' *Journal* as the perfect example of timely social satire.

Gens de Justice (The Lawyers) became Daumier's most famous series, in which he brought to life Molière's, Dickens's, and other writers' attacks on the quality of justice. Thirty-nine lithographs (D 1337-1377) between March 1845 and October 1848 were the result of Daumier's love-hate relationship with the law. The very attire of the French barrister must have attracted Daumier's eye. The contrast between the flowing black robe and the white neckerchief, topped with an arrogant face and crowned with a lawyer's wig, brings satire to life. Daumier's satire reached its apex of realism and artistic balance in *The Great Staircase of the Palace of Justice* (D 1372).

By 1841 Daumier had moved with his wife to the Ile Saint-Louis, even today a haven of pleasurable solitude within the bustling city. He was to remain there until 1863, working in an attic atelier. His personal world was circumscribed by that island and the tight circle of his inspired and often polemical friends, the only ones who appreciated his artistry—Delacroix, Courbet, Daubigny, and Corot.

The revolution of 1848 disturbed the idyll of Ile Saint-Louis but restored the freedom of the press when it dethroned Louis Philippe. Only two lithographs speak of the turmoil and of Daumier's steadfast republicanism, one of them entitled *The Final Council of Ministers* (D 1746, 9 March 1848). In it the old order flees in confusion before the glowing apparition of the republic. Unfortunately, the republicans were leaderless and divided, and the newly won freedom was soon frittered away. In two reliefs and several paintings, *The Fugitives,* Daumier showed the despair that followed.

In the aftermath of the upheavals Daumier also experienced a liberation of sorts. He broke out of the cycle of the weekly lithograph and into painting on a larger scale, so that most of his major paintings are dated after 1848. While the new political and artistic freedom lasted, new judges were chosen to apply better artistic standards to the Salon, whereupon he submitted to them a sketch entitled *The Republic:* a Mother Earth allegory, boldly outlining France nursing her children. Most viewers criticized it, but Jules Champfleury, surveying the dreary assortment of art work submitted, was an exception: "On that day I cried 'Long Live the Republic' because the republic had made a painter, DAUMIER" (*Oeuvres posthumes,* Paris 1894, p. 99). The monumental oil that Daumier painted from the sketch was called "heroic," as was the masterpiece that followed, *The Uprising.*[2] Overcoming the problem of adjusting to the scope of the canvas, he created a series of joyously lusty pictures, *The Miller, his Son and the Ass* and *Nymphs Pursued by Satyrs.* They recall Rubens's use of light. From now on, painting in oil became the emotional balance to the lithographic stone.

Soon the political climate changed again for the worse. Unemployment was rampant; starvation loomed; riots were suppressed by gunfire. Daumier mirrored the new climate in *The Representatives Represented* (D 1796-1885, November 1848-August 1859) and in a second, less pungent set of prints, *Faces of the Assembly* (D 1947-1978). A third set, *Parliamentary Idylls* (D 2050-2076, October 1849-February 1851), completed the series. The Second Republic barely had time to write a constitution when Daumier found a new subject, Louis Napoleon. Napoleon's nephew, brought back from British exile, soon outmaneuvered those who had planned to manipulate him and won a stunning victory by exploiting his uncle's name. In December 1848 he was overwhelmingly elected President. Victor Hugo gave blistering speeches and Daumier drew vitriolic caricatures. The masses, however, did not heed these warnings. Misled, they supported Louis Napoleon. Daumier was not fooled; once again he created a fitting reactionary symbol, Ratapoil. It represented the spirit of the times: arrogant, rakish, bigoted, narrow-minded, part Macaire, part Louis Napoleon. On the surface Ratapoil was inoffensively jovial, but as fashioned by Daumier in clay, bronze, and forty lithographs, he became menacing and sinister.

After three years of maneuvering, finding no more constitutional avenues but counting on the millions of Ratapoils, Louis Napoleon executed his *coup d'état* 1 December 1851. Troops appeared from nowhere and the faint begin-

---

[2]The authenticity of *The Uprising* has been questioned, and Howard P. Vincent avers that the work remained unfinished and was touched up by another hand.

nings of resistance were hacked into submission. Louis Napoleon had gauged his Ratapoils correctly; two weeks after the coup he was elected Emperor by an even larger majority than that for his presidency. Soon a new act of perfidy enraged Daumier. Louis Napoleon sent a French army into Italy to fight Giuseppe Garibaldi, who was fighting to liberate Naples from King Ferdinand II. *King Bomba, Le Roi de Naples* (D 2142) was Daumier's devastating judgment, showing the king surveying his realm of bombed-out buildings and corpse-littered streets.

It was not a time for artistic bravery. Louis Napoleon put Count de Nieuwerkerke, who detested Courbet and Millet, in charge of the Ministry of Fine Arts. Renewed censorship promptly followed. Hugo escaped to Belgium; Daumier was forced back into social satire. He repeated earlier themes and used a looser technique in sketches that he called *croquis,* emphasizing a main point rather than details. Some of his delightful social observations stem from this period. But despite their comic character, their poignancy or candor, the subjects were unworthy of Daumier's artistry.

Times were getting worse; the quality of paper at *Le Charivari* was deteriorating, making for poorer reproductions of his lithographs; and his Paris was disappearing as the picturesque winding streets of the *quartier latin* fell victim to the wide new boulevards designed by Louis Napoleon and his city planner, Baron Eugène Haussmann. In one of his most poignant lithographs, *Behold, our Nuptial Chamber* (D 2429), an elderly couple watches their home being pulverized.

The art world did not escape Daumier's withering crayon, nor did fellow painters or prudish audiences. His favorite subject, however, became the theater. He visited it often and was well-known to directors and actors. No niche remained hidden from his penetrating sight, whether yawning musicians in the pit, brawling spectators in the gallery, leering habitués in the parquet, fake stage drama, backstage backbiting, or the side-show barkers—*les saltimbanques*—advertising their wares in time-honored exaggeration. He noted the pompous aging tragedian, the fatuous gestures of inept performers, and the public's boredom with Corneille and Racine. Some of his most startling *chiaroscuro* emanated from the darkness of the house against the brightly lit stage. In 1852 he created one of his largest series, thirty lithographs and twenty-three wood engravings, all on the theater.

Even now Daumier's talent was hardly recognized. Weary of repetitive drudgery, he left *Le Charivari* in 1860; freed from lithographic commissions, he could devote himself to painting in both oils and watercolors, although the loss of his steady income at *Le Charivari* required a move to less expensive quarters in Montmartre. In the 1860s he achieved mastery in his oil paintings, notably

Third Class Carriage, The Print Collector, and *The Connoisseur.* From then on, in oils such as *Advice to a Young Artist* or *The Three Lawyers* he approached the brilliance of Adrian van Ostade and Rembrandt and the realism of Georges de La Tour. Manet and Monet, criticized by many and admired by a few such as Baudelaire and Zola, became Daumier's friends. His personal fortunes improved. Critics began to speak of him respectfully, even admiringly. Young artists visited him, and his work began to find buyers. Although by then he preferred to paint, he began to sell occasional lithographs to *Le Journal amusant.*

In 1862 Philipon died. That same year Daumier returned to journalism as a collaboraor on a new paper, *Le Boulevard.* But his continuing poverty forced him to return to *Le Charivari* in 1863. In 1864 collectors began to buy his paintings. Champfleury published a book on the history of caricature with an entire section devoted to Daumier, to which Baudelaire contributed a poem. As a result of these developments, Daumier moved from Paris to the village of Valmondois in the Oise Valley. Here he drew over two hundred lithographs for *Le Charivari* and *Le Journal amusant,* mainly an animated mélange of social caricatures.

In 1865 Louis Napoleon, now old and ill, relaxed the press laws. Immediately aware of his new freedom, Daumier left social mores behind and turned his crayon again to political issues. His last six years were an artistic triumph of political cartooning on an unprecedented scale. What accounted for his growing apprehension were the government's militaristic interventions in Italy and Mexico, its domestic stranglehold, and its lack of attention to the growing strength of Prussian-dominated Germany. Dissent could no longer be silenced, and the censor allowed both critical speeches and Daumier's grim cartoons.

One of the most delightful and shrewdest of the regime's critics was a cellist-turned-composer, Jacques Offenbach. In his *Orpheus in Hades* and *The Beautiful Helena* he not only succeeded musically but also made sly fun of the government while remaining safe from the censor, since his quipping and sniping were draped in antique garb, as Daumier's social satire had been earlier. His attack on the stupidity of the military in *The Duchess of Gerolstein,* as hilarious as it was malicious, found an echo in the audience's guffaws, Daumier included.

Daumier's style had become simpler and more intense. He now shaped bodies and events in their essentials only, bare of ornamental details. Symbolism began to take the place of personalities, with only an occasional recognizable face such as Czar Nicholas or Bismarck. War, Death, Peace, Liberty, the Monarchy, and Europe were his metaphors. As he continued to mirror the human comedy and tragedy he grew in concept and execution, if for no other reason than that lithography now repeatedly served him as a parallel study to his oils.

He had matured to the point where his cartoons became art rather than satire or caricature.

On one subject Daumier saw less and less need to be subtle — the growing menace of Prussia. Although he still dealt in symbols, depicting the danger from the east as a monster, a snake, a strangler, his artistic voice became bolder with every lithograph. He now warned of the inevitable collision and of the ineffectiveness of piecemeal French diplomacy. He personified Europe balancing herself precariously on a bomb whose fuse was burning low (D 3566), and France and Germany playing Gaston and Alphonse as they are about to enter *Le Bureau de Désarmement* (*"Après vous!"*). At the same time he kept his eyes on the home front and its machinations. The lithograph of the influential politician Louis-Adolphe Thiers shows him in a theatre-prompter's box directing the play without being observed, an apt stroke. No less pointed is his lithograph of a blind woman carrying a paralytic on her back towards a precipice.

True to Daumier's fears, Prussia invaded Alsace in 1870. In the ensuing war, France was crushed: Louis Napoleon surrendered and the Prussians occupied Paris after one hundred and thirty days of siege. Daumier's pictorial comments culminated in the lithograph of a grinning, beflowered Death figure playing the dirge *Dies Irae* on a double shawm amid the corpses of the battlefield (D 3854). In a gesture of pseudo-liberalism, the regime offered him the cross of the Legion of Honor. He refused. With nearly half of France occupied, the newly formed Commune and the rearguard of monarchy and clergy fought each other. Daumier followed the events, labeling the reappearance of the clergy as the Prussian occupiers left, "One invasion replaced by another." *The Empire Means Peace* (D 3814) is another sardonic comment. As France mourned her dead, he drew the epitaph *Dismayed with her Heritage* (D 3838). His lithographic valedictory was *The Monarchy is Dead* (D 3937).

The date of Daumier's last lithograph under contract with *Le Charivari* was 24 September 1872.[3] There was to be little more, because his eyesight was diminishing. He lived comfortably for seven more years after his retirement, honored in 1878 by the great showing of his work at the gallery Durand Ruel, and surviving to see the firm establishment of the Third Republic. He died 10 February 1879.

*   *   *   *   *   *

[3]Contrary to common belief, *The Monarchy is Dead* was not Daumier's last lithograph. Between 1874 and 1879 he drew a limited number (D 3938-3954). Fourteen were published in *Le Journal amusant,* one in *Le Charivari* (D 3946), one in *Petit Journal pour rire* (D 3952). One remained unpublished.

The lithographs of Daumier cast a never-ending spell intensified by our knowledge that these cartoons had the power to anger and embarrass kings and politicians. The man who drew them was not a firebrand. While his friend and contemporary Delacroix wrote copiously on subjects ranging from art to society, Daumier never sought such public outlets. His sword was the lithographic crayon, his battlefield the weekly picture he created.

After the youthful impulse to resist authority, which had landed him in jail, Daumier moderated his rebellion. When political regimes threatened harsh reprisals, he resorted to social satire, returning to political satire once censorship was relaxed or a regime toppled. At these moments of political change, the contrast between Daumier's heroic and non-heroic selves becomes evident. In his four thousand lithographs and one thousand woodcuts we witness the strong feelings that he expressed only in art, not in everyday life. He is lighthearted even in a letter written in prison. Friends and drinking companions remember that his casual comments were whimsical and aphoristic, never as heated as his pictorial comments.

The photographs and portraits of Daumier reinforce his outward placidity. In contrast to Gauguin, who left a banking career to flee to Tahiti, Daumier was the typical bourgeois. In contrast to the mental anguish of Van Gogh's life, Daumier's temperament was mild and untroubled, except for occasional worries about money. His married life was calm. Gentleness and tranquility are the features of Jean Feuchère's lithographic portrait of Daumier at twenty-two, his hair flowing romantically. Benjamin portrays a more realistic and sturdier Daumier at thirty, sporting sideburns, goatee, and a wisp of mustache, with top hat and pipe, indistinguishable from thousands of other *citoyens,* the only identifying mark a folio bearing the name Robert Macaire. A few years later, a caricature by Etienne Carjat depicts a long-haired Daumier with palette and brushes in one hand and a painter's staff poised like a lance in the other. Finally, Daubigny's warm noble portrait shows Daumier in still later years, his hair almost white, his dim-sighted eyes peering into the distance. These portraits give us few clues of the inner man, but rather intensify the contrast between his outer anonymity and his fiery spirit.

The distinction between Daumier's treatment of satire and humor is another important contrast. He was capable of effective, eloquent, and stinging satire. But he also knew how to use playful humor: the vanquished victor Menelaus, the blind and aged Narcissus, the domestic intrusions into a poet's life. Daumier is most delightful on the subject of music and musicians, with barely a satiric wink. In non-musical episodes he depicts musical "honors" for a deposed minister, Macaire "embellishing" music, an artist's "reception" for a visiting bourgeois. Exploring this neglected aspect of Daumier's art is not an easy task because, in contrast to other professions on which he lavished his wit in large series, musical subjects are, with a few exceptions (*Les Musiciens de Paris, Croquis musicales,* and *Etudes musicales*), strewn throughout his work and can be found in such diverse lithographic series as *Actualités, Les Philanthropes du jour, Voyage en Chine, Scènes d'atelier, Histoire ancienne,* and others. Seldom does he employ musical themes for political satire, reserving them for social caricatures which are no less telling.

What makes for immortality in a man who, throughout most of his life, was underrated and considered only an illustrator and cartoonist? The answer lies in universality. True, he was by his own account a man of his time, but so were his fellow illustrators at *Le Charivari,* who are now known only to the specialist. Daumier remains important to historians who value the authenticity of his details, but he has attained artistic eminence as well because of his lively imagination in creating timeless, recognizable images that make sense without the captions. In *The Legislative Belly,* for example, even if the caricatured figures of the Assembly are unknown to us, we can identify self-aggrandizement, torpor, indulgence, sloth, and indifference, and draw our own parallels. The very mastery of the art of satire robbed Daumier for decades of the right to be considered an artist. His art was too real and too practical. He was neither romantic enough nor eccentric enough to be compared to the masters. But at the extensive exhibit of 1878, one year before his death, the aged Daumier was finally given his due; the press sang his praises as an artist, describing him as "a great master of form" and his work as of "almost classic nobility and grandeur."

Baudelaire defined Daumier's style as "sureness of touch. He draws as the great masters draw." The lithographic stone demanded a combination of swiftness and unerring detection of the significant detail that could be caricatured. In the political lithographs, we are stunned by the artist's rage, passion, and power. When Daumier's satire gives way to humor, what attracts and affects us deeply is an inner life, a glow which he imparts to his figures as if he wishes them to enjoy a lust for life even as he makes fun of their shortcomings.

It has often been said that the drudgery of producing lithographs under contract stifled or at least retarded the noble ambitions of Daumier the painter. Others insist that his own indignation at oppression and hatred of injustice betrayed him into the drudgery of lithography. Still others argue convincingly that a more practical factor often kept Daumier from painting: the high cost of materials. The pressures of both poverty and politics may have impelled him to stay with lithography, but to today's viewer, an incomparable artistic *oeuvre* was the result.

Moreover, the theory of the frustrated painter is spurious. Are Rembrandt's etchings less inspired than his paintings? Are Goya's terrifying *Desastros de la*

Guerra inferior to his oils? On the contrary, their fervor makes them master-pieces of style and content, and this is equally true of Daumier's graphic works. In his four thousand lithographs we do not see the tired results of labor at a hated task. The glow, power, and humor are evident. Daumier held up the ideals of free men as a mirror to his contemporaries, a perpetual reminder that liberty is constantly threatened. Daumier the satirist, the "man of his time" who challenged the terror of his day, was also the immortal master who spoke of perennial aspirations, giving everyday events timeless relevance.

What makes it art? The unblinking eye, the unfailing hand, the illusion, the symbol. The combination of these ingredients enabled Daumier to create anything he might wish to satirize. The sparser the line, the greater the impact. Be it La Poire, Robert Macaire, Ratapoil, Death, or music, the symbol was understood. His symbols stood for his time and remain for all time.

E. G.

The Plates

1

Here comes the wild, tumultuous
Grand Galop!
Follow the crowd! Come to the office
and get your subscriptions!*

*A fanciful advertisement for the newspaper *Le Charivari*.

Del. 558
279 × 214 mm.
Le Charivari 1 May 1839

Lith. de Caboche Garneray et Cie

2

PARIS MUSICIANS

A modern Paganini, burning his
toupee in the heat of performance.

Del. 922
229 × 177 mm.
La Caricature 7 November 1841 and
Le Charivari 9 February 1843

Chez Bauger & Cie Editeurs, Rue du Croissant 16.

Imp. d'Aubert & Cie

Paganini moderne, se brulant le toupet, dans le feu de l'execution!

3

IN THE STUDIO

A polite way of getting rid of a
bourgeois patron: play him the same
melody forty-seven times in a row.

Del. 1723
252 × 195 mm.
Le Charivari 1850 (April or earlier)

Chez Aubert & C.ie Pl. de la Bourse, 29.

Imp. Aubert & C.ie

Manière polie de mettre un bourgeois à la porte d'un atelier, lui jouer quarante sept fois de suite l'air de la Monaco.

4

ADDICTION TO (DEPARTED) SPIRITS

GENUINE TABLE-LEVITATION.

Del. 2405
199 × 256 mm.
Le Charivari June 1853

Maison.Martinet, r. Vivienne 41 et 11 r. du Coq.

Imp. Ch. Trmocq Cour des Miracles, 9. Paris

La véritable danse des tables.

5

MONOMANIACS

THE AMATEUR GUITARIST

Defying everyone's yawns
As he sings his puny verse,
He would sing a parlor-song
On the ruins of the universe . . .

Del. 861
232 × 198 mm.
Le Charivari 2 January 1841

Chez Bauger R. du Croissant 16.   Chez Aubert gal. Véro-Dodat.   Imp. d'Auber &.

LE GUITTARISTE-AMATEUR.

Narguant le baillement immense
Qu'il provoque en chantant ses vers,
Il chanterait une romance,
Sur les débris de l'univers......

6

Firewood is expensive
and art doesn't sell.

Del. 146
198 × 222 mm.
Le Charivari 6 May 1833

Courtesy of Benjamin A.
and Julia M. Trustman
Collection of Daumier Prints
at Brandeis University

Le bois est cher et les arts ne vont pas.

7

CURRENT EVENTS

A new Count Almaviva trying to seduce
Rosina: Véron delivering a serenade
on the tune "Long live the King!"

Del. 2110
256 × 210 mm.
Le Charivari 21 May 1851

Chez Aubert & Cᵉ Pl. de la Bourse 29 Paris.

Paris. Imp de Mᵉ Vᵉ Aubert 5. r. de l'Abbaye.

Un nouvel Almaviva venant essayer de séduire Rosine - Véron en lui donnant une sérénade sur l'air de **Vive Henri V**.

8

PROFESSORS AND BRATS

A young man trying to learn
what are commonly called the social graces.

Del. 1466
192 × 241 mm.
Le Charivari 4 June 1846

PROFESSEURS ET MOUTARDS.

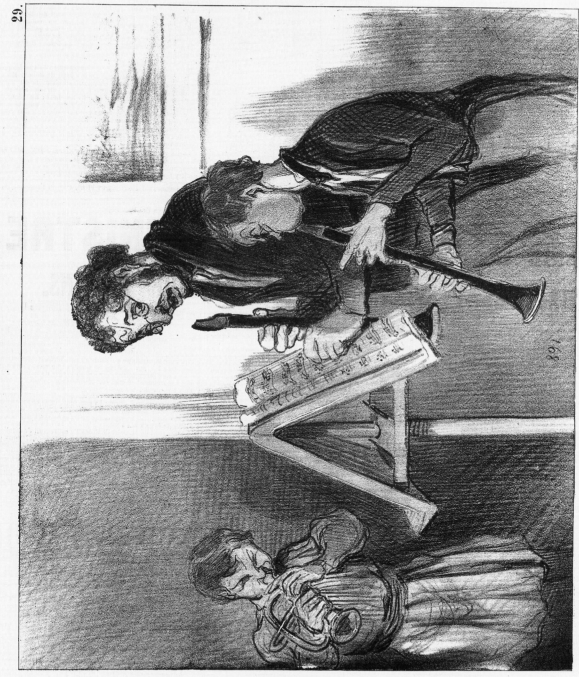

Chez Aubert, Pl de la Bourse, 29.

Imp. d'Aubert & Cie

Un jeune homme en train d'acquérir ce que l'on est convenu d'appeler un art d'agrément.

9

CURRENT EVENTS

Dr. Véron, the impresario, having renounced his
pretensions of politics, retires to the country
where he indulges in the favorite pastime of the
ancient shepherds of Arcadia: The true sage
consoles himself with philosophy and a clarinet.

Del. 2257
257 × 220 mm.
Le Charivari 25 June 1852

Imp. Mourlot F^res

Le Docteur Véron ayant renoncé à la politique à ses pompes et à ses œuvres se retire à la campagne à Auteuil et s'y livre aux divertissemens favoris des anciens bergers de l'Arcadie : le vrai sage se console de tout avec de la Philosophie et une clarinette.

10

CURRENT EVENTS

Mr. León Faucher, on leaving his house,
insists on receiving the honors
to which ousted cabinet ministers are entitled
by the decree of Messidor, year VIII.

Del. 2163
228 × 257 mm.
Le Charivari 31 October 1851

ACTUALITÉS

AVIS
PORTEFEUILLE
PERDU

H. Daumier

Chez Aubert & C.ᵉ Pl. de la Bourse de Paris

Imp. Ar. Frinoq Cour des Miracles 9. Paris.

Monsieur Léon Faucher tenant à se faire rendre, à la sortie de son hotel, les honneurs accordés par le décret de Messidor an VIII
aux ministres dégommés.

11

CURRENT EVENTS

PEACE—AN IDYLL.

Del. 3854
235 × 184 mm.
Le Charivari 6 March 1871

Courtesy of Museum of Fine Arts, Boston

12

THE GREAT DAYS OF ONE'S LIFE

BACK FROM THE FAIR AT ST. CLOUD

Down with penny whistles and those who
use 'em. How can such an instrument be
allowed in a country where the
clarinet is now accepted!

Del. 2263
225 × 218 mm.
Le Charivari 25 October 1845

LE RETOUR DE LA FOIRE DE St CLOUD.

Au diable les mirlitons et les mirlitonneurs.... comment peut on permettre un pareil instrument dans un pays ou l'on tolère deja la Clarinette!....

13

ANCIENT HISTORY

VIRGIL'S SHEPHERDS
(to a well-known air)

These beautiful children of Italy
Are constantly praising
The woods, the hill, the meadow
And the gentle sky which gave them birth.
Words and music by F. Beral

Del. 972
225 × 194 mm.
Le Charivari 11 December 1842

LES BERGERS DE VIRGILE.
Air suffisamment connu.

Ces beaux enfans de l'Italie
Célébraient ainsi tour à tour,
Le bois, le côteau, la prairie,
Et le doux ciel qui leur donna le jour.

(Paroles et Musique de Mr F. Berat.)

14

PHILANTHROPISTS OF THE DAY

Sir—here's what we are giving this year
as premiums for subscribers to *The Musical Universe:*
125 albums . . . eleven portraits of Mr. Musard . . .
three trumpets, with some keys missing . . .
forty concert tickets . . . 87 scores . . . and one penny whistle.

Del. 1316
227 × 172 mm.
Le Charivari 7 January 1845

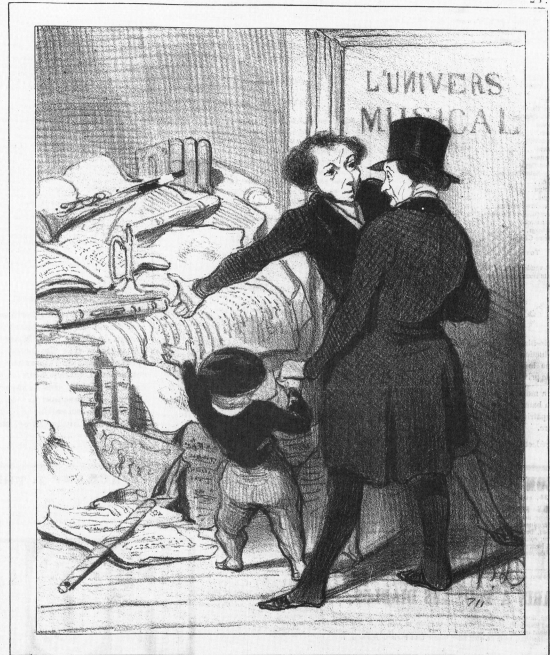

Chez Aubert & C⁹ᵉ Pl. de la Bourse 29.

Imp. d'Aubert & Cⁱᵉ

Monsieur... voici ce que nous donnons cette année en prime aux abonnés de **l'Univers Musical**.....
cent vingt cinq albums que vous pourrez faire relier plus magnifiquement les uns que les autres ....
onze portraits de Mʳ **Musard** à des âges différens mais toujours avec le même habit noir .... trois
trompettes plus ou moins à clefs....quarante droits d'entrée et même de sortie pour chacun de nos
concerts....quatre vingt sept partitions...et un mirliton.

15

TRAVEL IN CHINA

THE MUSIC LESSON

The Chinese man of means
likes to spend his leisure time studying music.
He takes lessons on the clarinet, accordion,
or hunting horn, and despite the dissenting
opinions of his unfortunate neighbors he persists
in calling this an agreeable pursuit!

Del. 1204
183 × 224 mm.
Le Charivari 24 October
and 6 November 1844

Chez Aubert & Cie Pl. de la Bourse 29

LA LEÇON DE MUSIQUE.

Le Chinois ren'tier aime à occuper ses loisirs en cultivant la musique : il prend très volontiers des leçons de clarinette,
d'accordéon, ou de trompe de chasse et malgré l'opinion contraire de ses infortunés voisins il persiste à appeler cela **un talent d'agrément!**

Imp. d'Aubert & Cie

16

PARIS MUSICIANS

Toot, toot, tootle dee toot . . .
Will you shut up! My wife has a headache . . .
How can one do serious reading in such a din?
Stop it, my little boy has a bellyache . . .
Call the police!

Del. 920
221 × 185 mm.
La Caricature 24 October and
Le Charivari 4 February 1843

Chez Bauger & Cie R. du Croissant 16.   Imp. d'Aubert & Cie.

.... «Ton, ton, ton, ton, ton taine, ton ton....» — Vous tairez-vous ! — Ma femme a la migraine. — Lisez-donc un drame
en cinq actes avec un orchestre pareil. — Finissez-vous mon petit a la colique. — A la garde ! — «.....Ton, ton,
ton taine, ton, ton.......»

17

THE BARKERS

Here you see the great celebrities
of literary, musical, and artistic France.
Their fame is all below sea level . . .

Del. 620
263 × 226 mm.
Le Charivari 5 April 1843

LES SALTIMBANQUES.

Vous voyez ici les grandes celebrités de la France littéraire, musicale et artistique, ils ont tous 36 pieds au dessous du niveau de la mer.

18

MUSICAL STUDIES

THE LAST VIRTUOSO ON THE TAMBOURINE.

Del. 3391
162 × 238 mm.
Le Journal amusant 9 December 1865

Courtesy of Benjamin A.
and Julia M. Trustman
Collection of Daumier prints
at Brandeis University

ÉTUDES MUSICALES, — par H. DAUMIER.

LE DERNIER JOUEUR DE TAMBOUR DE BASQUE.

19

CURRENT EVENTS

What rotten weather to go out and
alert the troops!

Del. 2543
198 × 269 mm.
Le Charivari 5 January 1855

ACTUALITES

Maison Martinet, 16 r Rivoli et r Vivienne

Lith Destouches, 28 r Paradis Pre Paris

h D —

720

L.D - 2542

— Quel fichu temps pour battre le rappel ! .....

PARIS MUSICIANS

—If you could only **C** how lovely
you are! (Pretend to play.)
—Hush! Soft pedal.
—You don't love me-**E**
—I mean to **B** your friend.

Del. 924
240 × 184 mm.
La Caricature 21 November 1841 and
Le Charivari 6 March 1843

Chez Bauger & C.ie Edit, R. du Croissant, 16.

Imp. d'Aubert & C.ie

— Si vous saviez comme vous êtes jolie! faites semblant de jouer. —Taisez-vous **do**. —Vous ne m'aimez pas **si**. —Et je serai toujours! **la mi**.

21

TRAVEL IN CHINA

AN ARTISTIC REWARD

The Chinese love music—but especially musicians,
and they carry this infatuation to extremes beyond civilized
nations' capacity to believe . . . If a pianist improvises variations
on a common tune like "Twinkle, Twinkle, Little Star" they bestow
upon him nothing less than a presentation sword,
which the recipient accepts with a composure equally laughable.

Del. 1209
216 × 188 mm.
Le Charivari 4 January 1845

Chez Aubert, Pl. de la Bourse, 29.

Imp. d'Aubert & Cie.

UNE RÉCOMPENSE ARTISTIQUE.

— Les chinois aiment la musique, mais ils raffolent surtout des musiciens, leur engouement en ce genre est porté à un point d'exagération qui ne serait pas compris dans nos pays civilisés; ainsi rien n'est plus commun que de voir des chinois s'atteler en guise de chevaux au cabriolet qui renferme leur idole et quand un pianiste a improvisé des variations quelque peu brillantes sur l'air du **Clair de lune, Ah! vous dirai-je maman**, ou autre **Roi Dagobert**, ils ne trouvent rien de mieux à lui décerner qu'un **sabre d'honneur** qui est offert et reçu avec un sang-froid également cocasse.

22

MUSICAL SKETCHES

The obligatory after-dinner morsel—the sonata
performed by the daughter of the house,
a young prodigy six years old.

Del. 2230
248 × 223 mm.
Le Charivari 11 February 1852

Courtesy of Fogg Art Museum,
Harvard University;
Gift of W. G. Russell Allen
and Paul J. Sachs

Chez Pannier & Cie rue du croissant, 16. Paris.   Imp. Ch Trinocq Cour des Miracles, 9. Paris.

Le morceau qu'on est obligé d'avaler après diner: _ sonate exécutée par la fille de la maison, jeune prodige agé de six ans.

23

MUSICAL STUDIES

THE ACCORDION, ALSO KNOWN AS MUSICAL BELLOWS

We don't yet have the right to kill people who play this instrument,
but let us hope the day will come.

Del. 3392
158 × 247 mm.
Le Petit Journal pour rire
9 December 1865

ÉTUDES MUSICALES, — par H. DAUMIER.

L'ACCORDÉON, DIT SOUFFLET A MUSIQUE.

— On n'a pas encore le droit de tuer les gens qui jouent de cet instrument, mais il faut espérer que cela viendra.

24

ANCIENT HISTORY

THE RESCUE OF ARION

This tenor, saved by a huge music-loving fish,
Owes his life to his lovely voice.
Many a famous singer of today,
Threatened in a similar way,
Wouldn't move the heart of an anchovy.

Quoted perhaps from Berlioz?

Del. 957
240 × 200 mm.
La Caricature 1 November 1842

er R du Croissant 16

Imp. d'Aubert & C.

LE SAUVETAGE D'ARION.
Par un gros poisson dilettante
Ce tenor fut sauvé grâce à sa fraiche voix.
Maint chanteur que l'Opéra vante,
Dans une pareille tourmente,
N'attendrirait pas un anchois.

Extrait d'un feuilleton de Mr Berlioz.

25

PARISIAN SOIREES

Musical evening: a great Italian aria
sung by a French amateur.

Del. 2352
200 × 273 mm.
Le Charivari 4 January 1853

1

453

Maison Martinet, r Vivienne, 41, et M. d' Oeq

Imp. Ch. Trinocq Cour des Miracles 4

Une soirée musicale. — Grand air italien chanté par un amateur français.

26

MUSICAL SKETCHES

A gentleman determined to prove
he can play and sing at the same time—
with awfully disagreeable results.

Del. 2233
247 × 218 mm.
Le Charivari 17 February 1852

Chez Pannier & Cie rue du Croissant, 16. Paris

Imp. Ch. Trinocq Cour des Miracles, 9. Paris.

Un monsieur tenant à prouver qu'il peut en même temps chanter et toucher du piano. — ce qui est un grand désagrément.

27

MUSICAL SKETCHES

A singer in the process of charming
the whole company with a popular song.

Del. 2244
251 × 219 mm.
Le Charivari 8 April 1852

Chez Pannier & Cie rue du Croissant, 16.Paris.

Imp.Ch.Trinocq Cour des Miracles, 9.Paris.

En train de charmer toute une société avec la romance du **Beau Nicolas**.

28

A COURSE IN NATURAL HISTORY

THE CICADA

The cicada belongs to the cricket family, which includes
street criers and some singers. You'll encounter her on the boulevards,
in cafes . . . even in many theatres . . . Her voice is off-key, shrill,
and resembles the scraping noise of a poorly greased cart . . .
One would gladly pay not to hear her . . . She usually ends up as
the lead singer at the Opéra Comique . . . Chances are she'll die of
hoarseness or perhaps a sixteenth-note stuck in her throat.

Fétis: *Natural History of Musical Creatures?*

Del. 530
215 × 190 mm.
Le Charivari 13 December 1837

Courtesy of Benjamin A.
and Julia M. Trustman
Collection of Daumier prints
at Brandeis University

mire dans tes yeux mes yeux......

La Cigale.

La Cigale appartient à la famille des cris-cris, des chanteuses à roulades, des grillons, des rossignols et des marchands de légumes. On la rencontre dans les promenades aux Champs Elysées, sur les Boulevards, dans les cafés, dans les Estaminets, dans les restaurants à 22ᶜ, dans tous les lieux publics, et même dans beaucoup de théâtres qui ne le sont guères. Sa voix est puissante, criarde, pointue, et ressemble au gémissement d'une charrette mal graissée. On l'emploierait très-utilement à crier au feu. On paie pour ne pas l'entendre. Elle finit ordinairement par être première Cantatrice dans quelque théâtre d'Opéra Comique à moins qu'elle n'ait commencé par là; c'est ad libitum. Enfin elle meurt d'enrouement ou bien d'une double croche rentrée, qui s'est mise en travers dans son gosier.

(Fétis, Histoire naturelle des animaux chantans)

13 Xbre 1837

29

THE GREAT DAYS OF ONE'S LIFE

ON THE CHAMPS-ELYSEES

A gentleman getting drunk on beer and music.

Del. 1183
240 × 228 mm.
Le Charivari 9 September 1846

Chez Aubert Pl. de la Bourse, 29.

Imp. d'Aubert & Cie.

AUX CHAMPS ÉLYSÉES.

Un monsieur qui s'enivre de bière et d'harmonie.

30

THE MIDDLE CLASS

The disadvantage of marrying a woman
who supposedly has some talent.

Del. 1553
238 × 198 mm.
Le Charivari 7 December 1847

Imp. Aubert & C.ie

Chez Aubert Pl. de la Bourse.

Inconvénient d'épouser une femme qui possède un talent dit d'agrément.

31

THEATRE SKETCHES

How a large family is useful to a singer.

Del. 2910
189 × 253 mm.
Le Charivari 28 January 1857

Courtesy of Benjamin A.
and Julia M. Trustman
Collection of Daumier prints
at Brandeis University

Imp. Martinet, 172, r. Rivoli et 41, r. Vivienne.

Lith Destouches, 28, r. Paradis P. Paris.

De l'utilité d'une famille pour une cantatrice.

32

CURRENT EVENTS

Her voice is certainly growing stronger.*

*The jester represents *Le Charivari*, observing and wryly commenting.

Del. 3717
238 × 203 mm.
Le Charivari 23 June 1869

Courtesy of Benjamin A.
and Julia M. Trustman
Collection of Daumier prints
at Brandeis University

LIBERTÉ

— Elle a décidément plus de voix.

33

AS YOU LIKE IT

The trouble with employing a servant
who once worked for the tenor Duprez.

Del. 1710
245 × 212 mm.
Le Charivari 28 March 1850

Inconvénient d'avoir des domestiques qui ont servi chez M^r. Duprez.

34

PARIS MUSICIANS

Chorus: "The sun shines so bright!" (aside: What a day!)
Chorus: "O my native Brittany, where glows the sun so bright . . ."
Hurrah for the composer, Loïsa Puget!

Del. 921
232 × 185 mm.
La Caricature 31 October 1841 and
Le Charivari 14 February 1843

Chez Bauger & Cie dit R du Croissant, 16.

Imp d'Aubert & Cie

(En chœur.) « Le soleil est si beau! » (à part) coquin de temps! (En chœur.) « Et puis de ma Bretagne...
le soleil est si beau!............. Vive Loïsa Puget!!!!! ....

35

THE GREAT DAYS OF ONE'S LIFE

A PUBLIC DECLARATION

—I lo-o-o-o-ve you . . .
—I lo-o-o-o-ve you . . .
(Since there's a flatted note in this tender avowal,
no husband can object.)

Del. 1174
240 × 233 mm.
Le Charivari 28 March 1846

Chez Aubert & Cie Pl. de la Bourse. Imp. d'Aubert & Cie.

UNE DÉCLARATION, EN PLEINE SOCIÉTÉ.

— Je t'ai ai ai ai me.......
— Je t'ai ai ai ai me!.......

(Ce tendre aveu se fesant avec un bémol à la clef le mari ne peut rien y trouver à redire.)

36

DRAWING-ROOM SINGERS

Woodcut (n.d.)

Les chanteurs de salon. — (Dessin de Daumier.)

37

MUSICAL SKETCHES

The music-loving family begins rehearsing at dawn
for its performance that evening
at the Knuckleheads'.

Del. 2240
249 × 213 mm.
Le Charivari 13 March 1852

Chez Pannier & C¹ᵉ rue du croissant, 16. Paris.   Imp. Ch. Trinocq Cour des Miracles, 9. Paris.

Une famille mélomane commençant à répéter dès le matin le grand morceau qu'elle doit chanter le soir au concert donné chez Mr Coquardeau.

38

MUSICAL SKETCHES

Parisian amateurs taking advantage
of Rossini's sojourn in Italy to perform
a selection from *William Tell*.

Del. 2229
248 × 223 mm.
Le Charivari 9 February 1852

Chez Panmer & C¹ᵉ rue du croissant, 16. Paris.

Imp.Ch.Trinocq Cour des Miracles, 9. Paris.

372

1443.   1853

Amateurs parisiens profitant du séjour de Rossini en Italie pour se permettre d'exécuter un morceau de Guillaume Tel!

39

A RECOLLECTION OF THE GRAND FESTIVAL
OF THE SINGING SOCIETIES

A view of the hall: plan, section, and
elevation of the conductors. A combination
of the arts of telegraphy and music.

Del. 3132
210 × 226 mm.
Le Charivari 2 April 1859

Courtesy of Fogg Art Museum
of Harvard University

SOUVENIR DU GRAND FESTIVAL DES ORPHÉONISTES

m⁰ⁿ Martinet, 172, r. Rivoli et 41 r. Vivienne.

Lith. Destouches 28, r. Paradis Pᵗᵉ Paris.

Aspect de la salle . — Plan, coupe, hauteur et élévation des chefs d'orchestre — *Alliance de*
la télégraphie et de la musique .

40

THE PHILANTHROPISTS OF THE DAY

Mr. Mayor . . . While passing through your city
we request your permission to give a big
concert for the benefit of the poor . . . All we
would take from the receipts are our traveling
expenses—which come to only 800 francs.*

*Box office receipts from a full house in the 1840s
would have come to about 1000 francs.

Del. 1309
238 × 193 mm.
Le Charivari 16 November 1844

Chez Aubert, Pl. de la Bourse, 23.

Imp. d'Aubert & Cⁱᵉ.

— Monsieurre le Maire... de passage dans votre ville nous venons vous proposer de donner un grand concert. **au bénéfice des pauvres**.... nous ne préléverons sur la recette absolument que nos frais de voyage,.. qui ne montent qu'à huit cents francs

41

MUSICAL STUDIES

Former recipients of honorable mention
at the Conservatoire.

Del. 3390
154 × 239 mm.
Le Journal amusant 9 December 1865
and *Le Petit Journal pour rire* (n.d.)

ÉTUDES MUSICALES, — par H. DAUMIER.

ANCIENS ACCESSIT DU CONSERVATOIRE.

42

MUSICAL STUDIES

Music for a country outing.

Del. 3389
150 × 242 mm.
Le Journal amusant 9 December 1865
and *Le Petit Journal pour rire* (n.d.)

Courtesy of Benjamin A.
and Julia M. Trustman
Collection of Daumier prints
at Brandeis University

ETUDES MUSICALES, — par H. DAUMIER.

MUSIQUE DE FÊTE CHAMPÊTRE.

43

MUSICAL STUDIES

The harp, a celestial instrument.
(Music Dictionary)

Del. 3388
166 × 247 mm.
Le Journal amusant 9 December 1865
and *Le Petit Journal pour rire* (n.d.),
the last line changed to *"Dictionnaire de Littré"*

Courtesy of Benjamin A.
and Julia M. Trustman
Collection of Daumier prints
at Brandeis University

ÉTUDES MUSICALES, — par H. DAUMIER.

LA HARPE, INSTRUMENT CÉLESTE.
(Dictionnaire de musique.)

44

RECOLLECTIONS OF THE SAINT-CLOUD FAIR

These musicians play for twelve consecutive hours
without asking for a raise in pay. Mr. Perrin, director of the Opera,
is thinking of making them an offer.

Del. 3378
169 × 244 mm.
Le Journal amusant 16 September 1865

N° 507. — 1865.

Rue du Croissant, 16.

LE JOURNAL AMUSANT

JOURNAL ILLUSTRÉ,

Journal d'images, journal comique, critique, satirique, etc.

Prix du numéro : 35 centimes.

16 Septembre 1865.

Rue du Croissant, 16.

PRIX :

3 mois. . . . 5 fr.
6 mois. . . . 10 »
12 mois. . . . 17 »

PRIX :

3 mois. . . . 5 fr.
6 mois. . . . 10 »
12 mois. . . . 17 »

SOUVENIRS DE LA FÊTE DE SAINT-CLOUD, — croquis par DAUMIER.

Musiciens jouant pendant douze heures consécutives à prix fixe, et ne demandant pas d'augmentation d'appointements. — M. Perrin, directeur de l'Opéra, songe à leur faire des propositions.

45

STREET SINGERS

Woodcut (n.d.)
224 × 160 mm.

Les chanteurs des rues. (Dessin de Daumier.)

46

PARIS MUSICIANS

"Where can one be happier
Than in the bosom of the family?"

These three artists would be happier in the bosom of
a pub, and their young recruit in the bosom of
a game of marbles.

Del. 923
332 × 190 mm.
La Caricature 14 November 1841 and
Le Charivari 20 February 1843

Pannier éditeur R. du Croissant 16.

Imp. d'Aubert & C.ie

« Ou peut-on être mieux   (bis)
« Qu'an sein de sa famille . . . . »

Ces trois artistes se trouveraient mieux au sein du cabaret, et leur jeune associé au sein d'une partie de billes.

47

MUSICAL SKETCHES

Obbligato preludes to any amateur concert.

Del. 2236
254 × 226 mm.
Le Charivari 3 March 1852

Chez Pannier & Cie rue du Croissant, 16 Paris.   Imp. Ch. Trinocq Cour des Miracles, 9. Paris.

Préludes obligés de tout concert d'amateur.

48

PROVERBS AND MAXIMS

An empty stomach is deaf to music.

Del. 803
232 × 186 mm.
Le Charivari 21 June 1840

Ventre affamé n'a pas d'oreilles.

49

SOCIETY COMEDIANS

The chamber group in a genteel household where they
indulge themselves by performing music-hall numbers.

Del. 3038
211 × 268 mm.
Le Charivari 20 April 1858

LES COMÉDIENS DE SOCIÉTÉ.

mᵉˢMartinet, 172, r. Rivoli, et 41, r. Vivienne.   Lith.Destouches, 28 r. Paradis, Pᵉ, Paris.

Un orchestre dans une maison très comme il faut, où l'on se passe la fantaisie de jouer l'opérette.

50

MUSICAL SKETCHES

The orchestra pit during the performance of a tragedy.

Del. 2243
261 × 216 mm.
Le Charivari 5 April 1852

Chez Pannier & Cie rue du Croissant, 16. Paris.

Imp. Ch. Trinocq Cour des Miracles, 9. Paris.

L'orchestre pendant qu'on joue une tragédie.

51

PARLIAMENTARY IDYLLS

"Far from parliamentary debate, young legislators,
Let's dance under the hazel trees.
Tircis with his bagpipes sings delightful tunes,
Let's dance, young legislators, under the hazel trees."

Ballad: Words by Mr. Vatismeni;
Music by Chevalier Riancev.

Del. 2052
208 × 274 mm.
PARLIAMENTARY IDYLLS Series:
Le Charivari September 1850 - February 1851

Loin des amendemens,
Jeunes Représentans,
Dansons sous la coudrette:
Tircis sur sa musette

Chante des airs charmans.
Dansons, Représentans:
Dansons sous la coudrette.
Romance.

(Paroles de Mr Vatismenil. Musique du chevalier Riancev.)

52

CURRENT EVENTS

The disciples of Mr. Cobdem* [*sic*] exhibiting to the Russians
the charms of peace through free trade.

*Richard Cobden (1804-1865), English economist and industrialist,
was an outstanding exponent of the idea of free trade.

Del. 2473
206 × 269 mm.
Le Charivari 31 March 1854 and
Les Cosaques pour rire (n.d.)

Maison Martinet r Vivienne 41 et 111 du Coq

Imp. Trinocq r du P.ᵗ S.ᵗ Martin, 113, Paris.

Les trois disciples de M.ʳ Cobden; se livrant à une dernière tentative pour faire apprécier aux cosaques tous les charmes de la paix.

53

ANCIENT HISTORY

SOCRATES AT ASPASIA'S HOUSE

A lover of wine and women,
Socrates, having supped, leaves wisdom behind,
And like a stevedore among party girls
Trips a light cancan.

Verse by Mr. Vatout

Del. 934
230 × 197 mm.
Le Charivari 5 June 1842

Chez Bauger R. du Croissant, 16.

Imp. d'Aubert & Cie.

SOCRATE CHEZ ASPASIE.

Aimant le vin et les fillettes,
Socrate après diner laissait sagesse en plan,
Et comme un Débardeur chez d'aimables Lorettes,
Il pinçait son leger cancan.

Poésies badines de Mr Vatout.

54

CURRENT EVENTS

HISTORY REVISED INTO MUSIC-HALL TURNS

Forward! King Arthur, Alexander the Great!

Del. 3679
244 × 239 mm.
Le Charivari 11 December 1868

Courtesy of Benjamin A.
and Julia M. Trustman
Collection of Daumier prints
at Brandeis University

L'HISTOIRE REVUE ET CORRIGÉE PAR L'OPÉRETTE

En avant deux Chilpéric et Agamemnon!

55

PARISIANS IN 1852

Music-Lovers' Row: snapshot taken at the Opera.

Del. 2220
256 × 219 mm.
Le Charivari 15 January 1852

Chez Pannier & Cie rue du croissant, 16. Paris

Imp. Ch. Trinocq, Cour des Miracles, 9. Paris.

Le banc des amateurs. — Vue prise à l'opéra.

56

MUSICAL SKETCHES

AT THE CHAMPS-ELYSEES

Is it the music that enables me to swallow the beer,
or the beer to swallow the music?

Del. 2231
255 × 211 mm.
Le Charivari 13 February 1852

Courtesy of Fogg Art Museum,
Harvard University;
Gift of W.G. Russell Allen
and Paul J. Sachs

Chez Pannier & C.ie rue du croissant, 16. Paris.

Imp. Ch. Trinocq Cour des Miracles, 9. Paris.

AUX CHAMPS ÉLYSÉES

On n'a jamais su si c'est la musique qui fait passer la bierre, ou si c'est la bierre qui fait avaler la musique.

57

MUSICAL SKETCHES

A VICTIM OF POLITENESS

Del. 2234
252 × 217 mm.
Le Charivari 26 February 1852

Courtesy of Fogg Art Museum,
Harvard University;
Gift of W. G. Russell Allen
and Paul J. Sachs

Chez Pannier & Cie rue du Croissant, 16. Paris.

Imp. Ch. Trinocq Cour des Miracles, 9. Paris.

Une victime de la politesse.

58

CURRENT EVENTS

AT MUNICH

After one hour of Wagner, under orders!

Del. 3650
238 × 214 mm.
Le Charivari 8 July 1868

Courtesy of Fogg Art Museum,
Harvard University

A MUNICH.

Après une heure de Wagner par ordre !!

59

SUMMER SKETCHES

An improvement for Paris theatres during the dog days—
fill the opera *baignoires** to attract an audience.

Baignoires means both side boxes and bathtubs.

Del. 3203
200 × 279 mm.
Le Charivari 16 and 17 August 1859

4.

m^{on} Martinet, 172, r. Rivoli et 41. r. Vivienne.

Lith Destouches, 28, r. Paradis P^{re} Paris.

Amélioration qui ne tardera pas a être apportée aux théâtres de Paris pendant la canicule.

60

MUSIC—PYROTECHNICAL, DIABOLICAL, AND HURLY-BURLICAL

. . . Macaire understands his time. We do not live in an age of
harmony. We want noise, lots of noise. That is why Macaire
. . . introduces fireworks and pistols into the symphony and makes
music to the sound of cannon . . . Notice is hereby given to
owners of outdoor cafés, holes in the wall,
and oases in the desert.

Del. 452
253 × 240 mm.
Le Charivari 11 November 1838

Par MM. Philipon et Daumier.   Chez Aubert gal Vero-dodat.   Imp. d'Aubert & C.ie

Musique pyrothecnique, Charivarique et Diabolique.

Simple ménétrier de bastringue, Macaire a compris son époque. Nous ne vivons pas dans un temps d'harmonie, il faut du bruit beaucoup de bruit! c'est pourquoi Macaire fait des vers charivaris, introduit les fusées et les pistolets dans la symphonie, et fait de la musique à coup de canon...... C'est plus ronflant, et surtout plus facile!...   Habitués des cabarets, cafés borgnes, Chefs d'établissements coulés, directeurs de concerts en plein vent, propriétaires de jardins déserts, Macaire serait votre dieu s'il enfonçait Strauss et Musard, comme il enfonça ses créanciers.
Baoued! Baoued! Pouff! Pouff!! Paaaouff!!!!